Original title:
Is Life the Answer to a Question I Didn't Ask?

Copyright © 2025 Creative Arts Management OÜ
All rights reserved.

Author: Sebastian Whitmore
ISBN HARDBACK: 978-1-80566-104-7
ISBN PAPERBACK: 978-1-80566-399-7

Unfathomable Depths of Living

In a world so bright, I ponder away,
Is this a game? Oh, come what may!
Chasing my tail like a dog on a spree,
Where's the owner? Could it be me?

I wake to the sun, a cheerful delight,
Only to trip over a shoe - what a sight!
Coffee in hand, spilling on the floor,
Guess it's just life saying, 'There's always more!'

I ask the stars for a little advice,
They twinkle and giggle, 'Oh, ain't life nice!'
But when I question the moon, he's silent and round,
Maybe he's tangled in thoughts yet to be found.

So here's to the journey, with fumbles and glee,
To leaping through puddles, oh, so carefree!
Life's a quirky comedy, a delightful jest,
Every stumble and giggle, I count as my best!

In Search of What Lies Beneath

I wander around with a smile wide,
Searching for answers that seemingly hide.
With every turn, a laugh pops out,
Life's quirky rhythm, it's all about.

Question Marks on a Blank Canvas

A canvas strewn with splashes and dots,
Questions high, but logic? Not a lot.
Pondering all while sipping my tea,
What's the question? Oh, what could it be?

The Enigmatic Tapestry of Existence

Threads of mischief weave through my day,
Tangled in riddles, I laugh and sway.
Each twist and turn, a giggle awaits,
Entwined in the chaos that fate creates.

Chasing Illusions Beneath the Stars

Under the sky, I chase a bright dream,
With stars that blink, they seem to tease.
Illusions dance like shadows at play,
While questions parade in a comical way.

The Gap between Knowing and Knowing

I ponder on a sidewalk bright,
With dogs and pigeons in a fight.
Is it the cheese that makes me smile?
Or simply wandering for a while?

Answers dance like moths at night,
While I just chase, it feels so right.
A knock, a door, and then I freeze,
Was I looking for some cheese?

Mirrors Reflecting What's Unasked

In mirrors I see all my quirks,
Reflections of my silly smirks.
What is the deep truth I seek?
Oh look, my hair has gone all sleek!

Do mirrors lie or just evade?
The questions pile, like socks mislaid.
Each glance reveals a new surprise,
A curious case of painted eyes.

Paths of Curiosity

I stroll along a busy lane,
With thoughts that dance like drops of rain.
Do ducks and cats have grander plans?
Perhaps they're plotting against my hands!

In this maze of whims and whys,
A squirrel shows the shape of flies.
Oh what is life, just silly games?
Where all the players share the names!

The Unseen Question Mark

There's a mark upon the page,
A mystery in my late-night rage.
What could it mean, this curve so sly?
Perhaps it's just my pizza pie?

Each bite is filled with cheesy dreams,
While logic twists like winding streams.
If all I ask is but a bite,
Then humor me and call it night!

The Focus of a Fleeting Moment

In a world of clocks that tick,
I ponder what I might have missed.
A dog in shades, a squirrel on a stick,
Is this reality, or just a twist?

I spilled my drink on yesterday's news,
The coffee's cold, just like my feet.
If life's a game, I've lost my clues,
Should I play hopscotch or retreat?

Transcending Unanswered Riddles

Why do we wear socks that don't match?
Is it fashion, or a pop quiz?
I laughed so hard, I've lost my catch,
Was it a joke, or just a whiz?

The cat's on the roof, or is it a dream?
My thoughts are dancing, out of line.
Do trees ever ponder their own theme?
I swear, this logic's gone divine.

Serenity in Abstruse Thoughts

If clouds wore hats, would rain fall dry?
I'd pay for answers—what a steal!
Trees whisper secrets, but oh, my oh my,
What do they know that we don't feel?

I tried to talk to my microwave,
It just beeped, like I was a fool.
In this wild ride, how do we behave?
Maybe it's best to just drool.

A Maze of Esoteric Thoughts

Chasing my thoughts like butterflies,
They flit and flutter, hardly stay.
Do fish dream deep, beneath the skies?
Or do they just swim, come what may?

I tied my shoes in a double knot,
And wondered if that would keep me safe.
With every step, I've lost the plot,
Join the circus, or find a waif?

Shadows of a Silent Yearning

In the fridge a long-lost snack,
I ponder where my days went slack.
A sock puppets' silent chat,
Sparks laughter in the midst of that.

Beneath the bed, my dreams reside,
With dust bunnies, they all abide.
A giggle masked behind the fear,
Do echoes find their way back here?

Patterns in the Chaos of Being

Life tosses confetti in the air,
Yet I trip on my own despair.
The cat holds court on the old rug,
While I sip coffee from a mug.

A puzzle piece stuck in my shoe,
Reminds me I'm a work in view.
Laughter dances in a spin,
As I search for my lost twin.

The Weight of Lingering Doubts

A scale shows all my hidden fears,
I hop on it, and it just cheers.
Bananas in the fruit bowl chat,
While the clock just ticks and laughs at that.

My plans play hide and seek in jest,
As socks unite for their own quest.
Confusion wears a silly hat,
And crumbs conspire against the mat.

Silent Scripts of Existence

A pen writes scripts I didn't choose,
As my thoughts, like sneaky cats, refuse.
Invisible ink spills from my mind,
While my coffee grows cold, left behind.

The calendar laughs with misplaced glee,
Wiping days like a memory spree.
With every twist, a chuckle peeks,
In the silent language that life speaks.

Chasing Shadows of Certainty

In search of answers, we roam all day,
While chasing shadows that twist and sway.
A cat chased its tail, oh what a sight,
Is that wisdom I seek or just a light?

Wisdom wears glasses, can't find her book,
I asked a goldfish, it just gave me a look.
Laughter erupts from this curious plight,
What's the punchline? Oh, that's just my plight.

Questions abound like balloons in the sky,
Floating around, I give them a try.
But like a balloon that takes flight too soon,
They pop with a giggle, a laugh, a tune.

The Uncharted Quest

We marched through the forest of doubt and fear,
Got lost in the woods, it's hard to steer.
My map was a pizza box, covered with grease,
Turns out the treasure was really just cheese.

With compasses spinning, we danced through the trees,
Hoping for answers that flutter like bees.
"Excuse me!" I yelled, "Can anyone guide?"
A squirrel looked back, then just ran to hide.

We stumbled on riddles and climbed every hill,
Found wisdom in jokes hidden under the quill.
But the quest for the truths still echoes and sounds,
As we laugh through the folly, no answer is found.

Questions Unraveled in Silence

I asked the stars, they just blinked in night,
Perhaps they're pondering their own blight.
A dog with a sock was my sage over tea,
He howled out my questions, then fell to his feet.

In silence, I ponder, did I miss the cue?
While socks on the floor have their own point of view.
The question remains like a ghost in the room,
But hilarity reigns in this search for the bloom.

With thoughts like confetti, all scattered around,
I laughed at the answers that never were found.
In riddles and giggles, I dance in delight,
For sometimes, the chaos turns darkness to light.

A Puzzle without Pieces

I opened the box, all edges and flair,
But puzzle pieces scattered everywhere.
I searched for the corners, the start and the end,
Turns out it's a puzzle that doesn't quite blend.

With pieces like socks, all twisted and stuck,
My mind raced with questions, oh, what bad luck!
Yet I found a laugh in the mismatched array,
Because mayhem's more fun than a structured ballet.

Every piece tells a joke or a tale,
As I try to fit square in a round little scale.
So here's to the chaos, the puzzlement's dance,
For laughter is better than finding a chance.

Where Curiosity Is Born

In a land where questions play,
And squirrels think they're here to stay,
The puzzled ants march in a line,
Wondering how they'll pass the time.

A cat with shades, reclined so cool,
Ponders deeply, 'What's a school?'
The fish in tanks raise fins to speak,
While pondering if they're all just sleek.

Balloons float by with secret dreams,
Waving gently, plotting schemes,
Each giggle and snort reveals the truth,
That laughter brings the joys of youth.

In this space of odd delight,
Unraveled thoughts take silly flight,
We jest and laugh, and ask the void,
'Is this confusion truly enjoyed?'

Threads of Uncertainty

A spaghetti mess of tangled dreams,
Life's a puzzle with missing themes,
The cat on a box, a sage in disguise,
Watches as clueless mice theorize.

With jellybeans stuck to the floor,
Questions bounce, yet answers snore,
A parrot squawks, 'What time is it?'
The clock winks back, a playful wit.

Colors clash in the morning light,
While shadows yield to playful fright,
Each twist of fate spins its own tale,
And laughter rides upon the ale.

So grab a cup and toast the dance,
Shake your worries, take a chance,
For in this chaos, we find our way,
Navigating the absurd each day.

Mirrors Reflecting the Unasked

In a hall of mirrors, all askew,
Reflections giggle, 'Who are you?'
A duck quacks wisdom, proud and fine,
While pondering if it's time to dine.

Questions hide behind ego's veil,
While answers float like a fairy tale,
With an elephant wearing a bright pink hat,
We wonder aloud, 'What is that?'

In the haze of whimsical thought,
The absurdity has us all caught,
Chickens debate if they should lay,
While pondering their role in the fray.

So peer closer and you might find,
Life's a riddle, hilariously blind,
Each twist and turn brings another joke,
Mirrors reflect—oh, the yoke!

The Dance of Hidden Realities

Upon the stage of life's charade,
Jesters dance in glittering spade,
With every twirl, they jive and sway,
Questions pirouette, come what may.

A turtle turtles with a clown's grin,
Pondering what's inside his din,
While iguanas invent their own beat,
And groove like kings—oh, what a feat!

In this theater of unseen play,
Every giggle brightens the grey,
The laundry sings as socks appear,
And dishes join in with each cheer.

So raise a toast to the untried jest,
To life's kooky quest, the vibrant fest,
In dance, we find the grace to laugh,
In hidden realities, chaos on path.

Embracing the Unsought Journey

With a map that leads me nowhere,
I stumble on paths unseen,
The compass spins in circles tight,
Laughing at what could have been.

I ask the trees where I should go,
They just rustle, shrug, and hide,
Each turn reveals a new surprise,
My fate's a rollercoaster ride.

I chase the clouds that float above,
Hoping to ride a silver line,
But they just beam and drift away,
I guess I'll just have fun, divine!

My shoes are worn, my socks are bold,
Adventure's calling, can't resist,
I'll dance along this jumbled road,
Life's punchlines tucked in every twist.

Residual Echoes of Regret

I made a choice, oh what a shock,
The pickle jar is now my throne,
Regretting all the pizza slices,
Yet here I am, a cheese-filled drone.

I ponder on the roads not taken,
Like socks that swirl in endless wash,
If life's a show, I missed a cue,
But what's the rush? I'm here to quash.

Regrets parade like clowns in space,
Wobbling on their unicycles,
Their laughter echoes in my mind,
But hey, it beats the dullicles.

Each missed chance is a punchline spun,
A jest, a quip, a giggly tease,
I'll wear my fails like badges bright,
And sip my doubts like fancy teas.

When Curiosity Dares to Wander

A question popped like popcorn hot,
Why is there jelly in a donut shop?
I roam the aisles of 'what ifs' wild,
With answers blurred, I grin and hop.

The fridge hums secrets in the night,
Like whispers of a midnight snack,
I chase the stars, with wonder bright,
Yet trip on questions in my track.

I'll chase the squirrels up in the trees,
And watch them plot their nutty schemes,
In every giggle, every breeze,
I find the absurd hidden in dreams.

Curiosity, a silly dance,
Twirling through thoughts both bright and bleak,
In laughter's grip, I'll take my chance,
And turn my wonders into cheek.

Serene Spaces Between Answers

Between the hush of thoughts and sighs,
I find a moment, wide and free,
Where silence holds its quirky throne,
And chuckles float, a symphony.

I pause between each pondered thought,
Like squirrels debating nutty schemes,
A giggle sneaks, then bubbles up,
In quiet spaces, laughter gleams.

With every pause, a silly wink,
The cosmos giggles at our fuss,
If answers hide in cosmic pranks,
I'll join the dance, not make a fuss.

Serenity rests in scattered laughs,
A treasure tucked beneath the weight,
So here I sit, in funny bliss,
Let's toast to questions we await.

Whispers from the Abyss

In shadows deep, the echoes dwell,
Questions swirl, like a magic spell.
I ask my socks, they laugh and flee,
The answer's lost, perhaps in tea.

A wise old cat sits on my chair,
Staring blankly into thin air.
I ponder deeply what it means,
But all I find are silly beans.

Colliding with the Unknowable

Bumping thoughts like bumper cars,
Lost in a galaxy of candy bars.
The cake asks me, 'What's on your mind?'
I shrug and say, 'A slice I can't find.'

Jellybeans dance on my desktop scene,
Who knew they'd have an existential gleam?
I ponder this while sipping tea,
And suddenly my toast starts to flee!

Glistening Hints of Forgotten Yearnings

A pickle jar whispers sweet regrets,
While my goldfish makes unexpected bets.
The blender hums a motley tune,
As I digress beneath the moon.

Forgotten dreams wrapped in a sock,
Chasing answers like a ticking clock.
But when I peek into the night's veil,
I find that cheese has set to sail.

The Allure of Unsought Paths

Chasing shadows on the wall,
Falling up, then taking a crawl.
Perhaps I should just nap a bit,
For answers hide where I can't sit.

My shoes have gone and formed a band,
Playing tunes on life's shifting sand.
While I ponder where to roam,
A taco truck feels just like home.

Beyond the Veil of Expectation

I pondered hard, where's the fun?
Expectations chase like a setting sun.
I asked the cat, she just stared back,
With moments lost in a playful snack.

The more I seek, the less I find,
Answers hide, like socks unkind.
A dog walks by, he wears a hat,
And winks at questions, just like that.

With every glance, the world confounds,
A fish can fly, it leaps and bounds.
Through bouncing doubts and giggles loud,
I dance with woes, I'm rather proud.

So here I stand, a jester's kling,
With laughter sharp, that's my main thing.
In merry thoughts, let chaos reign,
With riddles wrapped in bright champagne.

Answers in the Ripple of Time

I tossed a coin into the stream,
Hoping answers come with a gleam.
It splashed and danced, oh what a show,
I'm still unsure, where did it go?

The ripples formed a funny face,
As if to tease me, just a trace.
A duck quacked loud, 'What's your plan?'
While knitting socks, that's my grandstand.

Time flies fast, like a curious bee,
Buzzing questions around, you see.
I check my watch, it mocks my plight,
With every tick, doubts take flight.

In reflections deep, murky and bold,
Life's a jigsaw, stories untold.
I sip my tea, as hiccups chime,
Questions whirl in the march of time.

Wandering Through Unanswered Paths

With shoes untied, I roam the maze,
Where roots are puns, and time delays.
Each step I take, a misfit laugh,
I chase the road, a quirky path.

The trees debate with leaves of gold,
"What's the answer?" they subtly scold.
I ask a squirrel, he flips his tail,
"Life's a nut, don't turn pale!"

Yet still I wander, as clouds drift by,
With questions swirling, to touch the sky.
A rabbit hops, with glasses on,
And writes the plots to stories gone.

At every turn, a chuckle hides,
Among the riddles, wisdom bides.
So with a grin, I take my stance,
With every question, a silly dance.

The Language of Unspoken Dreams

In midnight whispers, shadows grin,
With secret dreams that dance within.
I speak to stars, they giggle bright,
With cosmic jokes in the velvet night.

The moon rolls over, with a flashy suit,
Winks at wishes, oh how acute!
I blurt my hopes in clumsy phrases,
While daisies bloom in laughter's mazes.

A dreamer's heart beats like a drum,
While pondering questions that leave me numb.
Yet somewhere deep, a sneaky thought,
"Maybe nothing is what I sought!"

So here's to dreams that waltz and sway,
In playful tones of a bright ballet.
I raise a toast with foamy cream,
To mysteries wrapped in an unspoken dream.

Voices of Unvoiced Doubts

In the morning light, I ponder and sigh,
Why do my socks always play hide and fly?
Coffee spills dance like a lovely ballet,
Where did I park my brain for the day?

Questions unspoken wander around,
Like a cat chasing thoughts, not a sound.
Did I forget to feed my goldfish again?
Or was it the plants? Oh, where have they been?

I trip on my shoelaces, a classic, you see,
Did I tie them too tight, or are they just free?
What if the moon is just cheese on a plate?
What's that smell? Oh no, it's a forgotten fate!

As I ponder these mysteries, I grin wide and bright,
Life's puzzling antics are a comedic delight.
Perhaps the joke is on me, oh so clear,
But laughter's the answer, and that's my career!

The Unwritten Dialogue

Conversations with walls are a curious spree,
They talk back so well, but I disagree.
In the fridge, leftovers wage a cold war,
Should I eat them today or just ignore?

The dishes are silent, in stacks they reside,
While laundry's on strike, it seems to abide.
Questions float gently in the air like a kite,
Would they answer me back if I thought hard tonight?

Why do I stand here with a sock on my hand?
Was I going to clean, or perhaps make a band?
Perhaps it's a riddle wrapped in a joke,
Or a wise cat's whisper, just a wily folk.

In the dance of the unspoken, I twirl and I leap,
Finding humor in chaos, like climbing a steep.
So here's to the laughter that keeps me afloat,
In this unwritten dialogue, a leaky old boat!

Embracing the Unknown

In the depths of the fridge, there's a mystery lurking,
Is it soup, is it sauce, or perhaps something jerking?
Embracing the unknown, I lift the lid high,
That's definitely not dinner, at least I can try!

In the garden of life, weeds plot and they creep,
While my flowers are snoozing in a colorful heap.
What if I talk to them, coax them to thrive?
Do plants have feelings? Let's ask the beehive!

Dancing with shadows on a Tuesday night,
Are they whispers of hope, or just lacking light?
What if my dreams are just bedtime reruns?
Do I chase the unknown or throw in my puns?

So here's to the quirky, the weird, and the fun,
Life's a circus act, and I'm on the run.
I'll embrace every chaos and laugh 'til I ache,
For the unknown's a comedy; that's a promise I make!

The Riddle of Existence

Beneath the stars, I ponder and twirl,
Why do I find crumbs in my messy swirl?
Do ants have a union, or just worker pride?
In the riddle of existence, do thoughts slip and slide?

Walked into a room, forgot what I sought,
Is it wisdom I'm missing, or just a thought?
Do socks need a meeting to discuss their flight?
Or are they just rebels, shrugging out of sight?

Pizzas spin tales, and my cat's on a spree,
Is he the philosopher? Oh, let's wait and see.
Dreams are like jellybeans, bright and bizarre,
Do they lead to the answer, or just leave a scar?

The riddle continues, with giggles and glee,
Life's a joke-telling, whimsical spree.
I'll laugh through the puzzles, the quirks and the fray,
For the riddle of existence is just here to play!

Whispers of Unformed Queries

In a world where questions dance,
Laughter fills the air, a twisted chance.
Do I seek the truth in the lost sock's flight?
Or ponder why my plants don't speak at night?

Did I ask my sandwich why it tastes so grand?
Or simply question if there's mustard on hand?
Balloons float by, full of unasked thoughts,
While cats wear hats, tying all in knots.

Spoons debate forks in a cutlery fight,
As I stare at the fridge, lost in its light.
Who's to say what questions I might hold?
When jellybeans whisper secrets untold?

In this circus of queries without a clue,
I consider if penguins dine on fondue.
Ticklish giggles echo through the air,
Where answers might lurk, but do I even care?

The Silence Between Thoughts

In the silence where my brain likes to hide,
A parade of confusions takes a ride.
Why do ducks waddle while chickens just cluck?
I search for old wisdom but find only luck.

An octopus juggles in my mind's endless sea,
While I ponder the meaning of toast with brie.
Does the moon ever wonder why it's up high?
Or is it too busy wishing it could fly?

Between each silly thought, I slip and slide,
As I wonder why my dog laughs when he tried.
If questions were cookies, what flavor would win?
I'd bake some for clarity, if I could begin!

Underneath all these giggles and frowns,
Are the voices of thoughts wearing mismatched crowns.
The silence tucks secrets between every word,
As I chase little giggles, absurdly stirred.

Unspoken Wonders

Beneath the stars, where wonders collide,
I ponder the fishes' laughter, their pride.
Do we need to ask if socks like to chew?
Or is that just the chaos of laundry anew?

The fruit bowl holds mysteries in its core,
Bananas debate if they're simply for more.
When life throws answers like water balloons,
Do we catch or let slip, with laughter and tunes?

Unspoken wonders flutter, a vibrant parade,
While my toaster dreams of a lounge serenade.
Are clouds here for mischief, or just here to tease?
As I giggle at shadows that dance in the breeze.

With humor tucked tightly In each silly nook,
Questions pop up like crazy in a book.
I chase after answers that play hide and seek,
Finding joy in the quirky, the unique.

Echoes of a Forgotten Inquiry

In the echoes of thoughts that bounce and fly,
I wonder if fish ever ask how to sky.
A gentle breeze carries whispers of glee,
As I ask the beetles, 'What's your degree?'

What if the toaster dreams of trips to the moon?
While the coffee pot sings an old morning tune.
Do turtles debate if they're really that slow?
Or are they just waiting for time to bestow?

The air is thick with giggles and sprightly air,
As I try to coax answers from thin, floating hair.
I ponder the wisdom of socks in a drawer,
And question if they dream of the ocean's roar.

As laughter erupts from the depths of my heart,
I invite my blunders to come and take part.
In the echoes of chatter where silliness sings,
I find joy in the questions that life sometimes brings.

In Search of Invisible Answers

I wandered through the aisles of thought,
Grabbing snacks, but answers I sought.
Beneath a pile of laundry old,
Was wisdom wrapped in socks, or so I'm told.

Questions danced like fleeting light,
In shadows thick, they took their flight.
I searched for clues in cereal boxes,
But found only crumbs—what a paradox!

A fortune cookie? Please, not a joke!
No wisdom here, just crumbs to poke.
I asked a cat, it just meowed,
Apparently, answers are to be avowed.

With each turn, the riddle spun,
Like a Frisbee soaring, never done.
So here I am, with thoughts afloat,
Chasing answers in a sinking boat.

The Dance of Untold Mysteries

The clock ticked loud, with secrets to prance,
Each second a step in an awkward dance.
I twisted my mind, wore mismatched shoes,
Seeking the rhythm, yet lost in the blues.

Tiny notes from shadows took flight,
Whispering truths that were just out of sight.
The moon played tambourine, oh what a sight,
While stars giggled softly, igniting the night.

If knowledge wore a tutu, it would twirl,
Around misconceptions that tightly unfurl.
With a bumbling grace and laughter quite loud,
I tripped on the cosmos, fell face-first to the crowd.

So let's cha-cha with questions unasked,
In a cabaret of riddles, all brightly masked.
Here in the farce, untold tales abound,
In the dance of life, answers can't be found.

Clarity in the Fog of Doubt

Amidst the fog, I squinted to see,
The answers lurked as shadows, oh fie!
I brought my flashlight and some snacks too,
But clarity refused, just a cloudy view.

I tangled with riddles, like hair in a breeze,
Between clumsy syllables, I fell to my knees.
"Hey, mister doubt!" I called to the haze,
"Could you point me somewhere? I'm lost in this maze!"

Fog giggled back, like a playful ghost,
Whispering nonsense, it gave me a toast.
I toasted with orange juice, confused as can be,
"To clarity!" I cheered, to the fog's glee.

But in this strange game, I learned to embrace,
The chaos of questions, the silliness of space.
And though no clear answers ever were found,
I danced with the doubt—what a joyous sound!

Where Curiosity Meets Ambiguity

Curiosity knocked on a door painted bright,
Ambiguity answered, a curious sight.
With a grin and a smirk, it tossed me a pie,
"Your questions are tasty, but do you want pie?"

With whipped cream questions piled high on the plate,
I forked my way through, feeling quite great.
But flavors were mixed, like a puzzle unmade,
Each bite brought more queries, I couldn't evade.

"Is this blueberry? Or maybe a prank?"
Ambiguity laughed, "Just take it, don't think!"
I chewed on the doubts, they crunched and they danced,
Questions twirled wildly; they seemed to have pranced.

In the end, with crumbs scattered wide,
I shrugged at the question, gave curiosity a ride.
For in each strange morsel, I found, oh so clear,
That asking too much can just bring more cheer!

The Treasure of Unmade Queries

In the attic of my mind, lost socks reside,
Among dusty whims and dreams, they hide.
Did I want to find the meaning of bees?
Or just the keys to my old release?

With each question left unasked, treasures swell,
Like the time I wandered into a cell.
Thought I sought wisdom, but where did it go?
Oh look, a cat! Just another show!

Should I inquire why birds insist on song?
Or is it better to sing along?
As answers parade in mismatched shoes,
I've learned some things, while losing the clues!

So I giggle at the paths that I didn't take,
For each twist and turn, I'm just wide awake.
Life plays a game with questions to lend,
But who needs them when jokes are my friend?

Specters of Potential Questions

Ghosts of inquiries haunt my days,
They float around in silly ways.
Why does my sock choose to take a trip?
Maybe it's seeking an oceanic slip!

What if I asked an auto mechanic?
For advice on love, isn't that manic?
Or ponder why pizza is square in shape,
When its toppings can easily escape?

As I guffaw at the thoughts that rise,
Are they mere jesters in clever disguise?
I find my joy wrapped in laughter's embrace,
Where questions pirouette with ridiculous grace!

In the end, I smile at the nonsense near,
For each unasked query, I hold dear.
The journey's more fun without the refrain,
Of answers that linger like forgotten rain.

A Tapestry of Untold Stories

Life spins tales without a script,
Like spaghetti twists when it's overwhipped.
What if unicorns crave tacos at night?
Or clouds are just chefs taking flight?

I wonder if astronauts tango with stars,
While sipping hot cocoa from candy bars.
Should I pester a cactus and ask it to dance?
Or let foolish dreams lead me by chance?

My mind is a stage for absurdity galore,
Where llamas wear glasses and plan to explore.
Tangled yarns of questions float by,
But why chase the clouds in a big pie?

In the web of thoughts, I twirl with delight,
Each thread is a chuckle, wildly contrite.
Untold stories shimmer, playfully bold,
As laughter dances where foolish dreams unfold.

The Intersection of Wonder and Doubt

At the crossroads where wonder takes flight,
Doubt wears a cap, looking quite polite.
Do ducks ponder about their own quack?
Or is that just a riddle on a snack?

Confetti of questions lands softly around,
As I trip over wisdom like it's unbound.
Should I ask an owl about who's wise?
Or just let my dreams spread their wings and rise?

With a tip of my hat to the musings unclear,
I applaud the absurdities that brought me here.
For every question hanging overhead,
A punchline waits, unspoken, unsaid.

So I dance in the realm where laughter flows,
And the truth is a joke that occasionally glows.
At the intersection where quirks collide,
I find my peace as the funnies reside!

Hidden in Plain Sight

A sock's on the floor, it clearly mocks,
As I search for my keys, and lose my thoughts.
The fridge hums a tune, like a jazz band tight,
While I ponder my goals late into the night.

In the cupboard, a spoon holds a meeting of fate,
Whispers of dinners gone by, the chance to relate.
Dust bunnies dance, forming groups in the air,
While I wonder aloud, was I ever quite there?

A cat on the sill surveys all with glee,
As I chase all my dreams, but where can they be?
The clock ticks and tocks, but what does it know?
Time's just a trickster, it puts on a show.

So I laugh at the questions that tumble like dice,
Finding humor in chaos, oh isn't it nice?
In a world full of riddles, I juggle with glee,
Hidden answers abound, if only I'd see.

Chasing Shadows of Certainty

A butterfly flits, with a wink from the sun,
While I flounder like fish, just looking for fun.
Is it safe to assume that the sky's always blue?
Each answer I chase leads to something askew.

The coffee's too strong, like a punch in the gut,
And the toast burns just right, as I'm deep in my rut.
If certainty's gold, I've found only dimes,
Like a clown on a tightrope, still searching for rhymes.

The fridge sings a song, 'bout what food I could make,
But I settle for leftovers, it's now or it's late.
These shadows that haunt, are they friend or foe?
In a circus of thoughts, it's the questions that grow.

So I dance with confusion, I twirl with delight,
In the chaos of life, I still find my sight.
With a giggle I ask, 'What was the quest?'
As the shadows of certainty, put me to rest.

Where Questions Linger

In a garden of wonders, weeds crop up with flair,
While I seek out the answers, that never quite share.
The dog digs a hole, unearthing my shoe,
And I ponder in humor, about what's really true.

Clouds float like marshmallows, fluffy and light,
But they cover the sun, and give me a fright.
I chase after thoughts, like butterflies bright,
Yet they flutter on by, just out of my sight.

A riddle once whispered, now echoes my past,
As I trip on the punchline, oh the die's been cast.
With laughter like bubbles, that rise and then pop,
I roll in mischief, and never will stop.

So I stroll through the hedge, where questions all drift,
Embracing the nonsense, life's ultimate gift.
For in all of this chaos, absurdly we cling,
To the joy that it brings, and the songs that we sing.

The Silence of Forgotten Yearnings

In the attic of dreams, where old clothes reside,
I find whispers of wishes, that once bloomed with pride.
A hat from the past speaks of places unheard,
While I giggle at thoughts that now seem quite absurd.

The chair creaks in laughter, it knows all my fears,
As I knit together a lifetime of cheers.
Old toys in the corner, they wink with delight,
'Take a chance on adventure, don't flee from the light!'

A mirror reflects faces, of who I might be,
Yet the ghost in the glass just chuckles at me.
I ponder the silence, the yearning, the fun,
As I channel the laughter, from things that I've done.

So I zip up my coat, and step out with glee,
Each moment a treasure, each glance is a key.
In the silence of longing, there's much to explore,
With a wink and a smile, what else is in store?

Engaging the Unanswered

In the fridge, I found a pie,
A mystery wrapped in a lie.
Whose is it? I dare to guess,
But all I find is sheer distress.

Questions float like balloons in air,
Should I pop them, if I dare?
Each thought spins, a wild fray,
Life giggles as I lose my way.

I asked the cat, but she just slept,
With twitching paws, secrets kept.
The toaster chuckled in the dark,
While crumbs held stories, oh so stark.

I scribble notes on napkin scraps,
Hoping for answers, maybe maps.
But laughter echoes, my brain's a mess,
As I dive deep into nonsense.

What Lies Beyond the Horizon

A squirrel steals my lunch one day,
Is it an omen? Who can say?
He stops and grins, then dashes fast,
While I just gaze, dumbstruck, aghast.

Beyond that hill, what could await?
A circus clown or just my fate?
I ponder deep, with furrowed brow,
Expecting answers, none here now.

The sun sets low, the shades grow long,
A saxophone plays a jazzy song.
Life's a dance of zig and zag,
While I sip tea from a paper bag.

Yet still I plot and scheme all night,
For dinners that never seem quite right.
The horizon winks, the moon shines bright,
And I just laugh, embracing the flight.

The Pursuit of Subtle Revelations

I sought the truth in a bowl of soup,
But just a noodle did I scoop.
The broth was warm, like a hug from mom,
Yet, questions lingered like a charm.

I chased my shadow down the street,
It danced and twisted, light on its feet.
It winked at me with a cheeky grin,
"Find what you're lost in, let's begin!"

A shoe with laces bold and bright,
Told me stories of the night.
And every step I took with glee,
Echoed laughter back at me.

In wobbly chairs, we plot and scheme,
Life's not a puzzle, just a dream.
With subtle jests and giggles galore,
I dive for answers, but find much more.

Dances with the Unknown

The clock ticks slow, as minutes creep,
A dance of uncertainty, can't help but weep.
The dog joins in, spins round and round,
While shadows chuckle without a sound.

A fridge magnet holds my dreams,
But all it whispers are silly memes.
The cat looks bored, gives a sigh,
"Why ask why? Just eat and try."

In the park, a child takes flight,
Chasing birds with sheer delight.
I join the fun, my worries fade,
In laughter's arms, I'm unafraid.

So I twirl with questions, wild and free,
The unknown's a dance floor made for me.
With each misstep, I find my tune,
As life hums softly, beneath the moon.

Seeking Solace in Uncertainty

In a world of puzzled grins,
I wander through my wobbly spins.
Questions float, like stray balloons,
I chase them all, singing tunes.

What is bliss? Is it cheese?
Or nap time under big oak trees?
Sipping tea, I sip in doubt,
While sunbeams play, and shadows scout.

Do ducks really waddle just for fun?
Or is there some deep reason spun?
I scratch my head, a grand charade,
Contemplating life as I lemonade.

Funny how wisdom sometimes hides,
In socks, in fridges, or in tides.
If only questions brought me peace,
I'd dine on cake and never cease!

A Journey through Unasked Questions

I set out with a curious mind,
Seeking treasures of the bizarre kind.
Each step a giggle, each turn a cheer,
Where did I park my thoughts? Oh dear!

A map of whims, a compass of sighs,
Each 'what if' is a surprise.
I wonder what I forgot to ask,
While tangled up in this merry task.

Could jellybeans hold the secret key?
To puzzle pieces, wild and free?
I dance with doubts, twirling round,
In the forest of questions that abound.

Then a squirrel tosses acorns from above,
As if he knows life is all about love.
With every leap, I chuckle and chase,
Finding laughter in this curious space.

Threads of Unanswered Thoughts

Tangled threads of thoughts I find,
Weaving stories in my mind.
What's the color of a sneeze?
Can laughter cure a million worries with ease?

I pose these queries to my cat,
Who twitches whiskers, and that's that.
"What's the deal with socks that stray?
Do they dream of getting lost all day?"

Mismatched pairs in a drawer parade,
Casting shadows in a shade.
With every riddle, I sip my brew,
Life's a circus, and I'm the star too!

With every giggle, the answers tease,
As if they're dancing in the breeze.
But rather than fret or seek to find,
I'll make a cake and unwind, unwind!

Fragments of Unvoiced Wonder

In a land where giggles roam free,
I ponder life like a bumblebee.
What if clouds are just puffy dreams?
Or what's the deal with spaghetti streams?

A dancing frog hops by my side,
With questions he cannot abide.
"Where do thoughts go when they flee?
Do they dive in puddles or climb a tree?"

Each fragment of wonder tugs at my sleeve,
As the sun winks and takes its leave.
Could whispers of doubt turn into cheers?
With laughter echoing through the years?

Let's gather the winks and chat with the stars,
While baking cookies with chocolate bars.
In this silly dance of pondering life,
I'll twirl with joy, forgetting strife!

Conundrums in the Quiet

In the stillness, I ponder, oh dear,
Why do my socks vanish, can you hear?
Perhaps they fled on a holiday spree,
Leaving me with one shoe, just me and my tea.

Do trees gossip when I'm not around?
Whispering secrets without making a sound?
Is the fridge alive, keeping food in a trance?
Or just a chilling beast, in a metal expanse?

If I chase the ice cream truck, will it stop?
Or will it just laugh, and go on to the top?
Life feels like a riddle, wrapped in a jest,
Yet here I am, craving that sweet, sugary quest.

Am I the navigator of this wild ride?
Or just a lone rubber duck, floating with pride?
In a sea of confusion, I might just embrace,
The fun in this puzzle, my own little space.

Searching for the Invisible

I looked for my phone, it sang a sweet tune,
Yet here in my hand, it's a ghost of a boon.
Did it hide in a sock or scoot under the bed?
It's always a game, with a twist in my head.

The keys took a vacation, I swear on my cat,
In the realm of lost items, they're having a chat.
A meeting of misfits, in the realm of the bizarre,
Where I'm just left wondering, 'Where's my car?'

Clouds drift like thoughts over skies full of haze,
Curling like noodles in a comedic maze.
Do they laugh at my search and my frantic little dance?
While I chase the invisible, missed every chance?

Maybe answers wear glasses, too thick for the sight,
Or dip off to dinner, in the middle of night.
I'll sip on some laughter, count giggles like sheep,
In my quest for the unseen, some joy I should keep.

Fragments of a Brooding Mind

Thoughts scatter like confetti, bright and bizarre,
Each piece a tale, like a shooting star.
What's hiding inside this tangled head?
Is it wisdom or whimsy, or just pizza bread?

I ponder my choices, like choosing a snack,
Should I dive into chips or just take a whack?
Life's a buffet, but I'm stuck in my chair,
As cravings do battle, life's a carnival fair.

Why does the toaster pop when I'm lost in my haze?
It's a judgmental machine, in a toast-filled craze.
Am I meant to be seeking, or just find a crust?
With breadcrumbs of laughter, that might be a must.

In every odd fragment, a giggle resides,
Life's quirks like confetti, like winking slide rides.
I'll gather the pieces, the smiles, the fun,
Embrace the absurdity till the day is done.

Uncharted Territories of the Soul

In the corners of my mind, maps fade away,
Navigating feelings like a game of charades.
Is that a flair for drama or just spilled juice?
Where's the compass for chaos, of which I might use?

Shall I dive into dreams, where cows leap and prance?
Or sip on my coffee, while taking a chance?
Each thought's a ticket, to a ride not quite real,
With popcorn and laughter, I cannot conceal.

Perhaps I'll explore through a realm of delight,
Where socks wear sunglasses and dance in the light.
Life's just a puzzle, with pieces all tossed,
In this playful adventure, we find what's not lost.

So here in this journey, I waltz with a grin,
Through uncharted territories, let the fun begin.
With humor as my guide, I'll wander and play,
In the land of the quirky, come what may.

Echoes of Thoughts Left Behind

In corners of my mind they play,
Echoes of thoughts that drift away.
I ponder while my socks don't match,
A riddle wrapped in a sleepy snatch.

Do I need a manual to get by?
Or just wing it, like a bird in the sky?
Questions bubble like a pot on the flame,
Yet my coffee's cold, and it feels the same.

What's the meaning of socks on the floor?
They've surely wandered from their drawer!
I'll chase them down with a laugh in my chest,
Declaring this chaos as quite a jest.

So here I stand with my thoughts in tow,
An amateur detective in the morning glow.
Life's quirky riddles are a curious game,
Perhaps it's meant to be wild and untamed.

Serendipity in the Mist

Woke up today on the wrong side,
But sunshine poured in like a goofy guide.
I tripped on my shoelace, then on my cat,
Fell into laughter, imagine that!

The toaster burned my bread again,
But found a donut hidden—what a friend!
A serendipitous snack on a foggy morn,
Reminding me joy is never forsworn.

Every stumble just a dance in disguise,
Turns out my breakfast is quite the prize!
Life wraps humor in clouds of surprise,
And laughter's the gift that never defies.

So here's to the moments that catch us unaware,
Life's silly quirks, showing that it cares.
In the mist of the day, let's have some fun,
With every mishap, let's laugh out and run!

Paradoxes of Being

Why do I wake up with hair on my head?
When dreams of styling filled me with dread?
I ponder the universe while I take a bite,
Of cereal swimming in a bowl of delight.

Oh, the paradox of eating to think,
While my thoughts drift off like bubbles that sink.
A tangle of wishes and whimsical dreams,
Floating through life on gossamer beams.

If answers elude like my misplaced keys,
Should I even bother? Just float on the breeze?
Comedy reigns in this perplexing whirl,
As I chuckle at life's fabulously twirled.

So here's to the mysteries that dance in the air,
Wrapped in absurdity, who needs to care?
With a wink and a nod, we'll figure it out,
In this playful paradox, we'll laugh and shout!

The Weight of the Unasked

Questions hang like laundry in the breeze,
While I sip my tea and scratch at my knees.
The weight of the unasked, a curious thing,
Like juggling fruit while birds start to sing.

I ponder the color of the sky at noon,
Do clouds ask each other, "What's our tune?"
My cat just yawns, oblivious and free,
While I'm stuck wondering if I should be me.

Is it heavy or light, this thought of a thought?
Like wearing a sweater that isn't quite caught.
With a grin I decide to dance with my doubts,
Spinning around, laughing, they're just little bouts.

So here we are, with a giggle and sigh,
In the weight of the question, let's leap and fly.
Every unasked query could tickle with cheer,
In the grand game of life, let's hold our ideas near!

Navigating the Labyrinth of Doubt

In a maze made of cheese, I wander with glee,
Questions float by like bees on a spree.
Each turn that I take brings more cheese to behold,
Yet the answers elude me, or so I am told.

I ask my pet goldfish, 'What's the meaning of fate?'
He bubbles and swims, as if it's too late.
Life's just a puzzle with pieces all wrong,
And I'm just the jester in this wacky song.

The walls of confusion are slippery and high,
I slip on some thoughts, and I start to fly.
Do the shadows have names, or do they just tease?
If only I knew, I could rest with more ease.

In laughter I sit, with my friends by my side,
We joke about truths that we try to confide.
The maze is quite funny, though questions abound,
Perhaps I'll just dance, and spin round and round.

The Echo of a Lost Query

I shouted a question into the vast sky,
It bounced back at me with a "Who am I?"
The trees chuckled softly, they knew all along,
No one really answered, just played a sweet song.

I pondered on riddles while sipping my tea,
The cup seemed to whisper, 'Just let it be free!'
The spoon gave a wink, 'Just stir up some fun,'
Life's less about questions, it's about the run.

An echo of laughter mixed in with my fears,
I chased after answers, but found only cheers.
What's greener than envy and sweeter than doubt?
Oh wait, it's just chocolate—there's no need to pout.

In circles I danced with my thoughts in a spin,
The heart of the matter resides deep within.
So here's to the questions that float in our heads,
Let's munch on bewilderment, and feast on some bread.

Foraging for Clarity in the Mist

In a fog with a fork, I search for a snack,
Looking for clarity, but I find just a quack.
The trees wear their blankets, the ground's slightly wet,
And I'm pondering mysteries, like my last bet.

A squirrel gives pointers, he seems a bit wise,
Nutty advice wrapped in fur-covered lies.
"Just gather some acorns, let worries fall slow,"
As I hunt for the answers, but find deep grilled dough.

Mists wrap around thoughts like a thick woolen shawl,
I joke with the shadows, let's have a good brawl.
Is it clarity I want, or just crumbs off the track?
I'll take a few chuckles, and call it a hack.

So I dance with the doubt, in my foggy delight,
With laughter as my compass and stars as my light.
For the answers are fickle, but joy's always near,
In foraging moments, I breathe in the cheer.

Faded Signs in an Abundant World

I wandered the streets, in a world full of flair,
With signs that said 'Yes!' but no one was there.
A billboard proclaimed, 'Most questions are wrong!'
Yet I couldn't remember what I wanted all along.

Balloons floated high, like my hopes on a string,
While pigeons debated the meaning of spring.
I tried to follow them, but they flew with such grace,
But missed all the fun—what a lovable race!

Graffiti of wisdom, splashed bright on the wall,
Promised free answers, but I found none at all.
"Just think of the donuts!" a passerby said,
"Or better yet, life's just a sweet piece of bread."

So I chuckled and danced, with my snacks in a sack,
In the abundance of wonder, I played my own track.
For life's not a riddle, just moments to share,
In the faded signs, I find joy everywhere.

другое

Do ducks have thoughts in ponds so deep?
They quack to each other, secrets to keep.
A frog leaps by with a grin on its face,
Maybe it knows the meaning of space.

In shadows, the beetles play hide and seek,
Each one a philosopher, clever and sleek.
They ponder the colors of leaves overhead,
While ants march in line, they're just looking for bread.

The moon winks down, full of quirky delight,
As stars giggle softly throughout the night.
But questions float up, like balloons in the air,
Who needs all the answers? The fun's in the flare!

Questions Drifting on the Breeze

A feather flies by, its journey unknown,
Does it wonder where it's drifted or flown?
Clouds are in whispers, with thoughts of their own,
But oh, what a game! Each breeze is a throne.

Do fish ride the currents, or just play the part?
In oceans of laughter, there's joy in the heart.
Seagulls are scribbling in skies high above,
Making their jokes, spreading giggles and love.

The sun yawns awake, with a chuckle it beams,
While shadows dance lightly, like sweet double-teams.
With every new question, more laughs will arise,
So let's drop our puzzles and just share the skies!

Silent Anecdotes of Understanding

In the corner, a cat naps with flair,
Does it dream of a world filled with fish and warm air?
While mice throw a party, all squeaks and delight,
They giggle at questions that fade into night.

Worms whisper secrets beneath leafy greens,
Are they telling tales of their wildest dreams?
With each wriggled wiggle, they laugh at our plight,
For wisdom, perhaps, is found in their flight.

The door swings open, old socks in hand,
Who knew they could travel to such a great land?
They tumble and twist in a world full of quirks,
Leaving behind only smiles and smirky smirks.

In the Wake of Echoes

When echoes come calling, they play hopscotch sweet,
In valleys of chuckles, where answers retreat.
Mountains hum softly with jokes of their time,
Making sure every whisper ends with a rhyme.

What is a cloud but a fluffy disguise?
With shapes of old tales and whimsical lies.
While valleys just giggle at questions we hold,
Each flicker of laughter, a story retold.

The horizon waves gently, adorned in bright hues,
Does it know the answers, or just hums the blues?
In the tapestry woven of laughter and cheer,
The fun is in living, not needing to steer!

Echoes of Unasked Whispers

In a world of chatter and cheer,
Questions fly like butterflies near.
I ponder what I did not seek,
As my thoughts dance and play hide and peek.

What if the sun forgot to shine?
Would we sip coffee or dine?
I look at my shoes, they make no sound,
Yet they lead me to places profound.

A cat on a fence gives me a wink,
Should I ask more, or just let it sink?
My mind's a circus, a wild parade,
As I trip on thoughts that won't ever fade.

I wave to the clouds, "Hey, what's the score?"
They float on by, leaving me wanting more.
I juggle the maybes, toss out the doubts,
Laughing at life, it's what it's about.

Unraveling the Known

A sock on my floor looks so lost,
In the laundry of thought, oh what a cost!
Do colors clash when they're in a spin?
Perhaps they whisper secrets within.

Around every corner, I find a fright,
A forgotten snack from last Friday night.
Beneath the muffin crumbs, there's a clue,
A breadcrumb trail, leading me to you.

Questions hang in the air like smoke,
Is this a joke? Or is it a poke?
My coffee spills while I'm deep in thought,
Maybe this chaos is what I sought.

A squirrel dashes fast, with a nut in its cheek,
Should I marvel at nature or seek out the sneak?
Life's odd little riddles tickle my mind,
In the comedy show, I'm the one left behind.

Secrets Beneath Each Breath

Tickle my thoughts beneath the sigh,
What do the stars hear when they pry?
Do they giggle at what's left unspoken?
Or whisper sweet lies, leaving me broken?

Each inhale's a secret just waiting to burst,
Like a balloon filled with curiosity first.
I chase down the answers on a fishing line,
But the fish keep laughing, 'You'll never find!'

Shadows stretch long at the end of the day,
They might offer answers or just lead astray.
With every chuckle, I ponder anew,
What's hidden beneath those skies so blue?

So here's a toast to the things we don't ask,
For laughter can hide behind every mask.
Let's spin in the wind like a leaf on the lawn,
For what's real isn't always what's gone.

The Unsung Inquiry

In the depths of a sandwich, what lies within?
The crusty secrets of where it's been.
Do pickles ponder if they'll be missed?
Or are they too busy in a briny tryst?

I race with my thoughts, they run in a pack,
While the answers elude me, no way to track.
What's the punchline to this cosmic jest?
Tomorrow's to-do list? Oh, what a mess!

Balloons hover high, caught in the breeze,
Whispering tales of the thoughts that tease.
Are they holding the truth, just out of reach?
Giving a lesson to those who still screech?

So here I sit with my questions in tow,
Like a clown on a tightrope, stealing the show.
In this swirling chaos, let's find the fun,
For the unsung inquiry is never quite done.

The Lingering Essence of Query

I ponder on my couch, remote in hand,
Can pizza be a breakfast food so grand?
With cereal on my mind, I laugh and sigh,
Should I ask the fridge, or just let it fly?

A sock strays from its pair, what a tale!
Is it seeking freedom, or lost on a trail?
The cat watches with a bemused delight,
Only to pounce when it makes a getaway flight.

Do plants ever wonder about the sun's ways?
Or do they just listen to the wind's praise?
A leaf turns, as though in deep thought,
Hints at the wisdom that nature has sought.

In the end, the questions may bring a snort,
For the answers are lost in a silly retort.
So I shrug at the wonder, pour another drink,
And laugh at the queries that make me think.

Footprints on Unmarked Paths

I wandered out in slippers, quite the sight,
Tripped over a pebble that gave me a fright.
Seeking answers in the garden so green,
I found the neighbor's cat who wore a crown, unseen.

Do trees laugh when the wind starts to tease?
Or do they just sway, pretending with ease?
I asked a flower, but it didn't reply,
Just bloomed and swayed as I walked on by.

Footprints leading nowhere, quite the riddle,
Was that a dance, or some cat doing a fiddle?
With curiosity, I step left and right,
But the path just giggles, fading out of sight.

Oh, to be lost on these unmarked trails,
Where life's secret whispers turn into tales.
Mischievous mysteries tumble and twirl,
As I trip through the universe, a dizzy whirl.

Searching for Clarity in Chaos

I searched for answers in my cup of tea,
And found a leaf that said, 'Just let it be!'
With every sip, a riddle does unfold,
Are the best stories just the ones we told?

Chaos reigns in socks that don't match,
Are they planning a heist? Time to dispatch.
The dog wags his tail, confused by my quest,
While I ponder the meaning of breakfast and rest.

Do rocks have opinions on the moon's glow?
Or is silence royal, with no need to show?
I asked a cactus, it pointed and pricked,
Told me to focus, but I just got kicked.

Amidst all the chaos, laughter rings free,
Questions abound like waves in the sea.
With no clear answers, let's dance for a while,
Finding joy in confusion, and laughter's big smile.

The Silent Language of Existence

Whispers echo in the halls of the mind,
Do squirrels ever ponder the acorns they find?
With a twitch of a tail, they scamper away,
Leaving me wondering what's left to say.

A philosopher snail moves at quite the pace,
In a world where time seems like a race.
With wisdom so deep, it travels the shell,
Leaving trails of thought in an arcane spell.

Birds tweet secrets that I can't quite hear,
Yet I laugh at the notion, sipping my beer.
Are they plotting a flight to a land of cheese?
Or simply debating the best time to tease?

The cosmos hums softly, a silent decree,
In the language of existence, just let it be.
With a wink and a nod, we dance through the night,
Finding fun in the questions, and delight in the light.

Ripples Through Time's Fabric

In a world where ducks wear hats,
I ponder if my socks were lost.
A time machine made of boiled macaroni,
Could it help me count the cost?

With clocks that tick in reverse,
And jellybeans that dance at night,
I question now if I should chase
The wisest wisdom — or just take flight.

Each ripple crinkles history's face,
While cats hold meetings in the sky,
Yet all I seek's a parking space,
To make my liquid lunch comply.

Oh, what a riddle wrapped in fluff,
Like bubble wrap that needs a pop!
The answers float, yet still I fluff,
As time keeps on, I dance and stop.

The Subtle Art of Not Knowing

At breakfast, cereal sings along,
With spoons that spin in dizzy glee.
I wonder where my coffee's gone,
Perhaps it's lost to whimsy's spree.

In clouds that look like bunnies' ears,
And fish that play the saxophone,
I question all my hopes and fears,
With answers made of sticky foam.

I'm wearing mismatched shoes today,
A fashion choice, or something more?
In this grand game of stitch and fray,
What's really worth the goofy chore?

Yet laughter, like a feathery pillow,
Wraps my confusion in its grace.
With every giggle, I feel less hollow,
In this wild, wiggly, messy race.

Harvesting Hints of Awareness

In gardens where the cucumbers chat,
And radishes recite old tales,
I dig for truths all dressed in sprat,
While penguins sail on tiny gales.

An acorn thinks it's bound for fame,
As trees set forth on journeys grand.
Yet I can't tell if it's a game,
Since squirrels hoard what's sidelong planned.

With clouds that giggle, skies that nod,
The sun sips tea with dandelions.
I pen my questions, strike a facade,
While wonder grows in playful pions.

Oh, farming thoughts that run away,
With pumpkins holding tête-à-têtes,
I chase those seeds of bright display,
Amid the laughter and the frets.

Blurred Lines of Understanding

When I walk lines that scribble fate,
With butterflies that wear tuxedos,
I get all mixed and try to translate,
The whispers of those tangled meadows.

A rubber chicken claims to know,
The secrets of my fishy dreams.
But every clue just seems to blow,
Like wind that teases ice cream beams.

In wobbly thoughts like jellied jam,
The yeses mix with nos in knots.
I chase the answers, yes I am,
While pondering the mystery of pots.

Yet in the giggles I discover,
A laugh, a wink, a cheeky nod.
Amid the chaos, I recover,
And find the joy that nature's trod.

Hidden Dialogues of the Heart

In whispers soft, our thoughts collide,
Like socks that hide from the laundry tide.
Do you ponder what's behind the door?
I thought I had a map, but I'm lost for sure.

We joke about life handing us lemons,
While I'm still baffled by my missing denim.
The heart speaks in riddles, quite absurd,
I ask for clarity; the silence just slurred.

In coffee cups, my dreams reside,
They're all mixed up like a botched ride.
A lurking question hides like dust,
"Who will pay the donuts?" is a must!

And if you ask me what's the score,
I'll chuckle and say, "I'm still keeping score."
With every yawn, I find a clue,
But the answer's lost and the coffee's too few.

Threads Woven in Mystery

A tangled thread hangs on my shirt,
Is it fate or just a quirk?
Each stitch a thought that falls apart,
In a game where I forgot my part.

Do socks converse when I'm not near?
Or comets giggle as they steer?
I stitch my dreams in hues so bright,
While wondering why the cat took flight.

In this fabric made of laughs and sighs,
My pants don't fit, oh how time flies!
I tailor questions to wear, so neat,
With mismatched patterns, they're quite the feat.

So here I sit, needle in hand,
Crafting answers I don't understand.
But isn't it funny, with each stitch I make,
I'm lost in a quilt of wonderful fake?

The Fabric of Unanswered Prayers

I folded my dreams with care and flair,
Hoping miracles would fill the air.
Instead, I got mischief, wrapped in a bow,
And a cat that thinks it's the star of the show.

With every whim and curious glance,
I ask for answers, but get no chance.
A blanket of wishes tossed on the floor,
Next to yesterday's cookies, who could ask for more?

There's glitter in my cereal, how quaint!
It sparkles like life—sometimes hard to paint.
I pray for wisdom, for wisdom to land,
But it seems my laundry's got more demands!

So here I ponder with socks mismatched,
And I laugh at the universe—what a catch!
For in every wrinkle and crease I find,
A puzzle piece of the funny kind.

The Maze of Exploration

With a map drawn by crayon, I venture forth,
Exploring the land of uncharted mirth.
Where's the exit? The question's great,
But first, let's snack—oh, this candy is fate!

In twisting tunnels of giggles and joy,
I chase the shadows, a curious boy.
Do the walls whisper secrets of what's ahead?
Or do they just hum tunes when I'm in bed?

I tumble through thoughts, both wild and wide,
With laughter as my compass, I take it in stride.
There's cheese on a pedestal, a sight so rare,
Is it a guidepost or a Feta flare?

So through the maze, with a hop and a skip,
I find joy in questions that make me trip.
A journey unfurling with twists asking why,
Yielding to laughter, alongside a pie.

Navigating the Sea of Ambiguity

Sailing on waves of glossed-over thought,
With questions untethered, yet answers are sought.
A compass that spins, where am I to go?
Maybe I'll find it by chasing my toe.

Waves crash with laughter, as I drift and I float,
While pondering donuts and dreams in a boat.
The wind whispers secrets, I can't quite discern,
But hey, who needs clarity? There's fun to learn!

Fish jump with riddles, they splash and they tease,
With every odd answer, I giggle and wheeze.
The sea's full of nonsense, I sail through the haze,
And shrug off the worries like sun-drenched days.

So here's to the journey, not knowing the cause,
As I chuckle at shadows that give me applause.
For in this sea's dance, where confusion is grand,
I'll laugh 'til I float, on this strange, quirky strand.

The Art of Unasked Wonders

In a gallery filled with quirky displays,
I ponder the paintings and strange little ways.
Each brushstroke a whimsy, unasked, just for fun,
Like a gala for thought, beneath radiant sun.

Shadows are mingling, they flirt and they wink,
Inviting me closer to sip from the ink.
What if I stumbled, with questions so grand?
Would answers come dancing, or take off, unplanned?

Oh, the sculptures of ponder, with laughter abound,
All crafted from wisps of what might not be found.
Yet here in this moment, I giggle with glee,
For unasked wonders are wild and so free.

So let's paint a future in colors unknown,
Where in joy, we can wander, and seeds of thought sown.

With whimsy our canvas, unframed, full of thrill,
We'll dance through the questions, no need to be still.

Eclipsed Queries

In a corner of cosmos, a question went black,
It danced in the shadows, then laughed at its lack.
I waved like a hopeful, attempting to see,
But eclipsed were the answers, like stars in a spree.

The moon wore a grin, as I stumbled around,
With quirks in the silence, where chaos was found.
"What's brewing with life?" my mind pondered wide,
But chuckles erupted from thoughts I can't hide.

Jupiter chuckled, "Just watch from afar,
For answers are tricky, like hitching a car!"
And Saturn chimed in with rings made of cheer,
"Sometimes the question's just why we are here!"

So I bobbed through the cosmos, with giggles and sighs,
Embracing the nonsense of starlit goodbyes.
In this dance of confusion, I floated so light,
Eclipsed but still shining, oh what a delight!

Unseen Truths

In the attic of thoughts, where dust bunnies play,
I searched for truths hidden, yet they ran away.
"The chase is delightful," they laughed with a wink,
"Why fret over answers when you can just think?"

The boxes of queries, stacked tall, in a row,
Each making me giggle, with their mysterious glow.
I peeked through the keyhole, oh what do I see?
A circus of ideas, all clamoring with glee!

The clowns of confusion performed on the floor,
While truths in disguise snuck out through the door.
I chuckled and twirled with the jester so bright,
For unanswered questions were pure giggly light.

So here in this attic, where nonsense takes flight,
I'll dance with the questions, basking in delight.
For unseen are the truths, in laughter we find,
That not knowing is splendid and joyfully kind.

www.ingramcontent.com/pod-product-compliance
Lightning Source LLC
Chambersburg PA
CBHW051659160426
43209CB00004B/953